THE ACTOR
AND HIS BODY

THE ACTOR
AND HIS BODY

by Litz Pisk

HARRAP LONDON

First published in Great Britain 1975
by GEORGE G. HARRAP & CO. LTD
182 - 184 High Holborn, London WC1V 7AX

ISBN   0 245 52707 9 (boards)
       0 245 52721 4 (limp)

Composed in IBM Journal by LMA Ltd., Southampton.
Printed in Great Britain by
REDWOOD BURN LIMITED
Trowbridge and Esher

FOREWORD

The January afternoon light fades in a church hall in North London.
The electric light stays off. In the centre of the room stands a kitchen
candle in a saucer — the sacred flame on an altar. On the floor sit a
group of a dozen or so women, the youngest eighteen, the oldest over
seventy. They are totally still for a long time. Then, one by one, they
come to kneel in front of the flame and, spreading their arms, they
open themselves to the God. Softly, their breathing becomes
rhythmic, and gently their bodies begin to move in ecstatic commun-
ion. When the circle is complete they breathe together as one.

It is hard to describe the impression that scene made on me. I was co-
directing with Casper Wrede a BBC Television production of Euripides'
Women Of Troy. It was the first time I had ever worked with Litz
Pisk. I had come out of Oxford University a few years before, and
like most with that background my theatrical consciousness was
largely literary, academic, abstract and physically totally inhibited. I
admired Sir Tyrone Guthrie for his stagecraft, and was beginning to
be influenced at second hand by the ideas of Michel Saint-Denis. Into
this sky Litz burst like a red comet. For her, I saw, the spiritual
and the physical were not divided. The highest ecstasy was dance. Her
impact was very great but not because she talked about it. She never
did. It was because in class and rehearsal I could see what she was.
Ever since then, every time I have worked with her, that influence
has steadily deepened and matured. It has been a constant inspiration.

Now that she has largely retired from the theatre the loss is irrepar-
able, but I hope this book may do something to soften the blow. It
has been eagerly awaited by all those who have worked with her, and
by those who only know of her great reputation. What it cannot
replace is the daily experience of Litz in the rehearsal room for those
of us who were lucky enough to see it. On those rare occasions when
she now appears the aura affects one as strongly as on the first day
one met her. There is a heavy stillness of personality, a meditative
gravity, a supreme self-discipline, and a contagious seriousness which
can create an atmosphere of deep concentration as if by magic, with
a glance of the hooded eyes and a half-lost mumble. And then
suddenly, when she seizes the back hem of her long skirt and pulls it
up through her legs to tuck it in the front of her waist to demonstrate
a movement, one experiences the elastic tension and the dynamic
power of an Indian temple sculpture.

But what is it that makes her so unusual to work with? After all, there are many talented choreographers. I think it is simply that she isn't a choreographer. The programme always says 'Movement by Litz Pisk'. Another of the great divisions under which we suffer is that between each of the arts. Straight theatre, opera and ballet speak entirely different languages. It was not always so. For the Greeks a 'foot' in metre was a foot — a step, and it implied a note. One of the greatest difficulties and one of the most urgent necessities is to re-combine the performing arts. This can only be done by going behind the disciplines to find a point at which they meet. This Litz always tries to do. For her the step comes last, and only as the final and outward expression of an inner impulse. Always she works from the impulse. When that is alive then it is possible for it to find form facially, vocally and physically. Thus the text, the acting, the music and the movement can have an organic relationship to each other, as can the specialists in each area. Litz and I, for example, can always discuss the emotional intention in detail first, where we speak the same language, before finding our different ways to express it.

Litz Pisk and I have worked together in many different contexts — at the BBC, at the Old Vic, at the Royal Shakespeare, at the National Theatre, at the English National Opera and at the 69 Theatre Company in Manchester. She was in charge of all movement for the last season at the Old Vic before the National started in 1962-3, when I was Artistic Director. I am of course only one of the many directors she has worked with in recent years. Before she came to England she was a designer as well. Her distinguished past abroad and her work with the Old Vic School, and latterly the Central School of Speech and Drama, are in many ways even more important as an influence on the theatre than the productions in which she was directly involved. She is a great teacher, and has changed many who will change the theatre.

Perhaps her work is most powerful when it is concerned with the divine or the demonic. No-one who was part of it will ever forget the rehearsals for the Troll scene in *Peer Gynt* at the Old Vic, with a large cast of actors of all ages and backgrounds, many with no training or experience of movement at all. Because her movement is always connected to an emotional intention she can perform miracles with the apparently hopeless physically as well as the extremely talented. But I suppose it is her ability to create a physical state of serene ecstasy that has most affected me. Her dance at the end of *As You Like It* at Stratford-on-Avon in 1961 was a hymn. At its best Litz's work has given me a strong sense of being an exile. In glimpses it has become transparent — a window into a different kind of life, that we might lead, or once led long ago. It fills one with yearning. Can art give a higher stimulus?

Michael Elliott

ACKNOWLEDGMENTS

Thanks are due to the following for their kind permission to print
the poem and extract detailed below:
St John's College, Oxford and The Hogarth Press for 'The Panther'
by Rainer Maria Rilke, from *Selected Works* Volume 2, translated
by J. B. Leishman.
Faber and Faber Ltd for permission to reprint 'Hawk Roosting'
from *Lupercal* by Ted Hughes.

We should also like to thank ILFORD Ltd and particularly
Mr E. G. Mercer — Principal of the ILFORD X-ray Centre,
Tavistock House — for spending so much time and care in taking
the splendid radiographs for this book.

CONTENTS

INTRODUCTION

The shape of your body and the way you stand, sit and walk
indicate your personality.
The motivations of your movements spring from physical, emotional
and mental sources and your actions originate in one, two or three
impulses.
There are many interactions and endless permutations.
Your body is cold and shivers,
you feel cold and are miserable,
you say it is cold.
Physical experience informs your feeling and your mind.
You are overwhelmed with joy,
your feeling overflows,
you jump, dance and sing.
Superfluidity of feeling bursts into physical activity.
You think yourself betrayed which causes an emotional disturbance
and induces you to shout and fight.
Thoughts prompt your emotions and actions.
Your brain has a very efficient system of telephone-communications
to and from all parts of the body. Divorced from the body your brain
becomes the great dictator, doubter and dissector who cuts your
body and its movements to pieces. The actor who says he has 'three
feet' and cannot do a certain, quite natural step indicates that the
intelligence of his body does not reach the foot, the limbs are not
coordinated with the centre, a branch inside his body is divorced
from the stem.
You feel your body. You are aware of its sap and of its ebb and flow.
You are conscious of its energy or lack of it.
On the physical level the shape of your body is the outer boundary
of inner contents. Movement which starts from an impulse and is
joined to the centre of the mover has the power to emanate.
Repetitive, purely physical exercising might result in a very efficient
technique or virtuosity but the actor's movement is not a virtuoso's
technique. The actor does not move for movement's sake and he does
not beautify movement for beauty's sake. If he is called upon to
dance he will do so as a certain character in a specific time, place and
situation. The actor's body may be small or big, short or tall and he
transforms his body into any body. He moves out of abundance and
need. He is centred in his own nature and is bound in relationships
to the centres of other natures.

Movement-practice is a freeing-process. Freedom here means the springboard, the point of readiness to bring yourself and your body into the service of acting.

First of all it is essential to allow your body to fall into passivity before engaging it in activity. The emphasis is primary on the downward- and secondary on the down-AND UPWARD-movement. Heaviness and lightness depend on how much weight moves towards and falls into the centre and how much rebounds and is lifted off the centre. The crescendos and decrescendos of the body are enormous and the degrees of slowness and quickness are infinite.

To become aware of an inner rightness you have to find the particular, and discover how the parts fall into their places and support each other and unite with the whole.

Movement and voice are naturally linked with the in- and out-going air of your breath. Reflex-actions and reflex-sounds often happen simultaneously. Change of physical condition and shape of body 'grow' different voices.

It needs stillness to become aware of your breathing-rhythm and your heartbeat-meter and of the smallest movements occurring within your body. In complete stillness the lightest and slightest movement breaks the surrounding space and stirs the air. A turn of the neck can be a big meaningful movement.

The body is three-dimensional and is meaningful in every part and from and in all directions. The back says as much as the front and it makes no difference whether you act in the square or in the round, in a set or in the open. Movement emanates from your centre to your periphery and beyond and shares itself out in space. Size of movement is easily reduced without loss of intensity but it is no good extending size by forcing it to become bigger. Impulse has its own specific size and length of movement in which it consumes itself. It is not the size of movement but its central impulse and degree of concentration which induce the power of penetration.

Through the experience of movement you become aware of false tensions and habitual interferences and discover how to conserve energy. The elasticity of your body enables you to preserve a surplus of stretch. When the two-way-traffic of movement from inside-out and outside-in flows freely the body gets out of the way and can give way to your imagination. With yourself and your body held in readiness your personal and as yet unknown invention and fantasy of movement come forth.

You have the power to make your body free and to integrate every part you liberate. You dare your body in action and let it be thrown in passivity. The experience of extremes helps you to realize the condition of equilibrium.

1 *AWARENESS*

You inhabit your body by your presence in it and by your awareness of it. You do not watch it from the outside, arrange yourself in front of the mirror, stand or walk next to yourself, observe and analyse, but connect yourself with your body and feel for an inner rightness. Awareness extends from the nakedness of your existence, devoid of any adopted attitudes. It starts with your breath, your pulsation and your feeling for your sap from the bones to the skin.

When you lie relaxed on your back and spread your weight evenly, you rely on the support of the ground and feel no need to lift or hold any part of your body. Nor is there any need to waste energy by lifting, holding, gripping, pressing, tightening or contracting to yourself when you stand. Inside your body all parts have a place where they belong and are at rest. The centre of each weight is balanced on the centre of its support and the whole of your weight is firmly planted on the ground. You can rely on the self-support of the body.

From the neutrality of the middle of placing and the middle of tuning, you alert yourself to distinguish every one note as distinct from the other and distinct from two or more joined or opposed movements. Movement starts centrally and works itself out. Every inner movement has an outer consequence. Movement is joined to the mover and he is sensitive to the touch of the false move like the musician's ear is sensitive to the false note.

You release movement by being aware of the heaviness of weight when lifted and you let all weight fall and allow weight to hang freely and swing from any fixed point in your body. You give in to the fall and rebound of weight and by doing so you release movement without push of energy.

You activate movement by working with intent and intensity to extend the elasticity of connective tissues, tendons, ligaments and muscles and to enlarge the movability and articulation in the joints. You turn inwards and feel how strength collects, and you turn far and wide outwards and feel how strength supports you and gives of itself.

You move in rhythm and beat of time and experience slow motion and speed and the control which holds the pause in perfect stillness. You rely on the air to cushion and to support you.

You move into space and discover your freedom within its dimensions by advance, retreat, curving, circling and also by taking any objects,

such as a chair, a pillar or a tree into your awareness.
You open out and meet the other creature, the other person, the many others. You make their existence present in your own and widen the possibilities of communication.

2 *THE SPINE*

Your movement-practice begins with your bones, their connective
tissues and muscles. The most essential part of your body is the
spine. It is as important to discover its parts as it is to unite the parts
with the whole.
G. K. Chesterton remarked, 'a strange idea has inflicted humanity
that the skeleton is typical of death . . . . (instead of) the essential
symbol of life.'
The spine is formed by 24 true and 9 false vertebrae. The true
vertebrae are separated by pads of cartilage (the intervertebral discs)
which allow movement. The 9 false vertebrae are fused and there is no
movement between them. The spinal cord is a stalk of nerve tissue.
The central nervous system includes the brain and the spinal cord.
Linked with the spine are the shoulders and pelvis. The way you lie,
sit, stand, walk, run, jump and fall is effected by the spine. Its
elasticity acts as a physical shock absorber.
The spine transmits to the spectator messages such as your being
tense or relaxed, tired or rested, cold or warm, old or young and it
assists to transform the shape of the body and the sound of the
voice.
Anatomically the parts of the spine are named:
a 7 cervical vertebrae
b 12 thoracic or dorsal vertebrae
c 5 lumbar vertebrae
d 5 sacral and 4 coccygeal vertebrae.
These I shall refer to as:
a the neck
b the shoulder- and chest-area of the spine
c the centre-spine
d the root, base or tail-end of the spine.
Linked with the spine are: the shoulder-girdles which consist of two
clavicles or collar-bones and two scapulae or shoulder-blades, the
chest or thorax and the pelvis, which I shall call by various names
such as the bowl, the seat or the hips.
Ball- and socket-joints connect the upper-limbs or arms with the
collar-bones and the lower-limbs or legs with the pelvis. A pivot-joint
balances and turns the skull on top of the vertebral column.
The spine influences the tuning of the whole body and if it is held
tense or stiff coordination and fluency are disturbed.
By retracing the way back to the spine before it has straightened

itself upwards you will gain or regain its movability and strengthen the contact with its components and the unity with the whole. Think of the snake, cat, monkey, the embryo and man.

When you work on movements which roll and unroll the spine, or bend and stretch the upperbody or let its weight fall and rise, make sure the head always lowers first on the downward-movement. The upward-movement should start from the base of the spine and end with the neck. Do not lift the head but wait until it is rolled up by the neck-vertebrae and stretched from the muscles at the back.

When the movements require you to stand always check on the position of feet and knees. The weight should rest on the heels and on the outside of the feet and the toes should grip the floor. If the feet are together the heels should almost touch each other and the toes should point slightly outward. Whether you stand with the feet closed or apart, or in a step-position, the knees should always point in the direction of the feet.

Most movements can be practised four to sixteen times except where the number of repeats is stated. All movements given here can be extended and developed further.

PRACTICE

Initial Movement

Stand with your feet about 12 inches apart and breathe in.
As you breathe out let your head, shoulders and spine drop
forward rounding the upperbody to yourself and bend the knees
slightly.
Breathe in as if yawning with and through the whole body, rise
and stretch yourself out. Do this without any consciously made
up-movements.
Release the stretch and let the breath go on the sound of
'Zzzzzzzzzzzzzzzzzzzzzzz' like the air going out of a balloon, and
collapse into as low a kneebend as you can, rounding the upperbody to yourself again.
Breathe in and repeat the yawning and stretching. Feel the sap
going through your body from the centre to the finger-tips.
Remain standing and grip the floor firmly with your feet. Lower
the arms and release the inner stretch slowly and sigh out on the
sound of 'Haaaaaaaaaaaaaaaaa'. Do not bend or drop forward or
backward or to the sides. Let the weight of every part of your
central body sink inwardly and become aware of how one part
comes to rest on top of the other. Feel for the base of the spine
and make sure your head is lightly balanced. Think of the root,
the stem and the crown.
As you stand upright close your eyes and sway a little forward
and backward. Slowly reduce the swaying until you come to a
complete standstill and open your eyes. Your body should be at a
right angle to the floor and you should look straight ahead. Try to
stand without holding, lifting or pressing and without consciously
positioning your body.

Roll and Unroll

Sit on the floor, bend your knees and let your upperbody drop
forward and inward.
Unroll the upperbody. Start from the base of the spine and lower
vertebra after vertebra until your whole back touches the floor.
Let your legs slip forward from the knees and outward from the
hip-joints and let your arms drop outward from the shoulder-
joints, letting them rest a small distance from the sides of your
body. Make sure the hands and feet are totally disengaged and the
neck and head are free.
Raise the head and shoulders and round the upperbody forward
and inward again. As you do this try to connect with the spine and
contact one vertebra after the other.

15

Unroll the upperbody back to the floor again. Practise this very slowly at first. When the unrolling and rolling up are smooth and even, increase the tempo.

When you lie on the floor feel for your total height from the heels to the top of the head, and feel for your width, sharing one half out to the right and one half to the left. Rely on the support of the floor and imprint this condition of letting go into your physical memory.

Slowly rise and stand upright. Recall from the horizontal position the openness of your body. Rely on the self-support of your body.

Round Hollow and Straight

1. Position yourself on hands and knees and hunch your back. Bend the tail-end of your spine down and in, round the centre-chest- and shoulder-spine and drop your neck and head. Make your back into as convex a shape as you can.
   Raise the tail-end of the spine, hollow the centre-chest- and shoulder-spine and raise your neck and head. Make your back into as concave a shape as you can.
   Lower the pelvis, straighten the centre-chest- and shoulder-spine until it is in line with the tail-end. Lower the neck just far enough to bring it in line with the shoulder-spine. Your back should now be parallel to the floor and as straight as a table-top, supported at right angles by your arms and upperlegs.

Practise these movements slowly at first. When they work well increase the tempo. After the last repetition loosen out. Wriggle with the whole spine, the shoulders, shoulder-blades and pelvis. Slow down gradually until you are quite still. Sit on the floor and release any strain or tensions in your arms and legs by shaking them out.

2. Kneel and lower your seat towards or on to the heels. Put your lower arms on the floor with the elbows near your knees.
   Round the whole of your back and tuck your head in.
   Move your back forward and stretch your neck until the chin is just above your thumbs.
   Stretch your elbows, move your back upward and straighten the spine.
   Move backwards, lower the seat, bend the elbows, tuck the head in and start again.

The movement of this sequence should be smooth and continuous. After the last repetition loosen out again. Sit on the floor and unroll your spine until you lie flat. Bend the knees and point them upwards. Wriggle with the spine, moving round, hollow and straighten it and finally curl into the embryo-position.

16

The practice of these movements strengthens the contact and enlarges the movability of the spine. The next movements are concerned with the self-support of the spine when you sit and stand.

3. Take an upright chair. Face the seat and sit astride it. Hold on lightly to the back of the chair with your hands. Move the base of your spine off the seat of the chair and let it hang freely.
   Lift the tail and hollow the centre of your spine. Take note that this is the wrong move with the intention of making you become more aware of the right one. Feel how the shaft is strangled in the centre. Watch for the neck to incline, to tilt back or overstretch to the front. Become aware that the root pulls out of the bowl and the stomach drops forward.
   Search for the vertebrae in the centre or lumbar region, move these slowly back and drop the tail-end. Feel for the root lowering. As you do these movements make sure not to round the shoulder-spine. The neck and head now move into line with the base of the spine. The pressure on the diaphragm is released and the stomach glides back into the bowl. Do not pull or press the soft parts in the front of your body but leave these totally disengaged and passive.
   Try to push the chair away and remain in the same position as you were when seated. At first you might find this difficult because of insufficient strength in the thigh-muscles but after further practice you will be able to do this quite easily.
   Slowly straighten the knees and stand. Make quite sure not to alter the alignment of the pelvis, spine and head.
Feel how the centre of one part is supported by the centre of the one below.

4. Stand with the feet about 12 inches apart. Bend the legs slightly and put your hands on the knees.
   Drop the head, round the spine and lower the tail-end.
   Raise the tail-end, hollow in the centre and raise the head.
   Drop the head, round the spine and lower the tail-end again.
   Unroll vertebra after vertebra until the spine is upright and straighten the legs. The pelvis should be in the same position as it was before and the neck should be in line with the base of the spine. The eyes should focus straight ahead. Check on the position of feet and knees and feel for the self-support of your body from floor to head.

17

Collapse into a Kneebend

Rolling and unrolling the spine

Round Hollow Straight

20

Round Hollow Straight

Pelvis lifted   **Pelvis dropped**

Round Hollow Straight

3 NON-RESISTANCE

Think of three movements:

a done to you; you are being punched and sink to the floor (this calls for your experience in falling into your own weight and demands your physical non-resistance).

b letting it be done to you; you lose all your strength and are dragged and flung about (this calls for your experience of total passivity and demands your absolute relaxation).

c doing yourself; you collect your strength, rise and walk away (this calls for your experience in the use of the rebound from the fall of weight and demands resilience of muscle).

Gravity and levity are correlated and are equally powerful. Resistance to gravity interferes with fluency because it makes for hard points, or knots or props, which do not allow the channels to be free for movement to travel to and fro and out or in. If you hold on to any part of your body and resist the fall of weight you cause tensions which shorten ligaments, stiffen muscles and use energy to no effect.

The downward-movement is naturally dominant in the practice for yielding to gravity. Muscles soften and joints hang loosely. This is a necessary transitionary condition for the body to get ready, similar to the kneading of clay before you start to work with it. The experience of the fall of weight into its own heaviness is very important. Weight can only rebound if it falls and it has to hang freely to be carried upwards and flung far by the swing.

It is obvious that it is in your power to isolate movement in one part of your body, or to act on one after the other, or to engage two or more, or all simultaneously. Every bit of the human body is expressive. In a sculpture the nape-line is as meaningful as a fist and your body is your own living human sculpture. The spectator who notices and puzzles over an actor's head and neck, constantly held to one side of the shoulders for no apparent reason, is distracted and unable to become involved in the more important happenings on stage. On the other hand, a chin which is pushed up, a stiff back, rounded shoulders, turned in feet and closed or open hands, are as telling as words when introducing a character.

Your practice should explore all possible movability of the joints but first every part should find its rightful place, its home from which to set forth and to which to return.

Any part which is lifted, held and tightened by habit is pulled out of

its natural place. By letting go and loosening out you juggle the parts into their natural places, release pressure on connective tissues and gain length of ligaments, tendons and muscles.
When practising the next exercises you work the movements locally, that is, disengaged from the rest of the body which should remain passive. This brings about more awareness and clarity and also economizes energy.

PRACTICE

Head and Neck

Stand with your feet slightly apart. If you are inclined to lift the tail-end of the spine, bend the knees a little and drop the pelvis. This releases pressure in the centre of the spine.

Let the jaw drop and the head sink forward and breathe out. Feel for the weight of the head. Let it hang loosely and shake it gently. Allow the jaw, lips, tongue and cheeks to vibrate and use breath-sounds.

Raise the head from the back of the neck and stretch the vertebrae up. Leave the chin, the area in front of the neck and the facial muscles disengaged. Move the jaw slowly up until lower- and upper-lips touch very lightly.

Sink the head to the sides and raise it.

Let the jaw drop and the head sink backwards. Make sure you leave the throat open and do not involve the shoulders.

Raise the head, move the jaw up and stretch the neck straight.

With one foot in front stand in a step position. The soles of the feet should be firmly planted on the floor and your weight-line should drop between the feet. Tap with the heel of the foot in front about 12 times, as fast as you can. If the head is lightly poised on a straight neck it should respond to the tapping with a vibrating movement.

Shoulders, Arms and Hands

1. Stand with your feet slightly apart and let your arms hang loosely at your sides.
   Pull both shoulder-balls up as high as you can. Feel the tension and the shortening of ligaments and muscles in the neck- and nape-region.
   Let the right shoulder-ball fall heavily down and allow the arm to sway. Then let the left shoulder-ball fall and the arm sway. As you repeat alternate the first fall. Make sure there is no pull or pressure on the neck, chin and jaw when the shoulder-balls fall. The shoulder-blades move up and down but the spine is not involved.

2. Pull both shoulder-balls up and let them drop to the front. The shoulder-blades open and the arms hang forward.
   Pull the shoulder-balls up again and let them fall backwards. The shoulder-blades close and the arms hang back.
   Pull the shoulder-balls up again and let them fall straight down.
   The shoulder-blades should be neither open nor closed but flattened towards the central structure.

3. Lift your arms straight up with the palms of your hands turned to each other.
   Pull the shoulder-balls up.
   Keep the arms up and drop the shoulder-balls. The elbows should remain straight.
   Lower the arms to your sides and as you do so shake elbows and wrists and loosen them well out.
   Imagine you have a cape or a shawl draped over your shoulders. Move only the shoulders and without the help of your hands shake the cape loose until it drops. (You can also do this with a real cape or shawl.)
   Make sure the shoulder-balls and shoulder-blades are well dropped down and the arms hang loosely at your sides. Check that the hands are relaxed, the palms are turned towards the thighs and that the fingers are uncurled.

Upperbody

1. Stand with your feet about 24 inches apart. Bend the knees a
   little.
   Let the whole of your upperbody sink forward and fall between
   your legs. Do this by dropping and rounding the neck-shoulder-
   and centre-vertebrae and then fall loosely from the base of the
   spine.
   Leave your upperbody hanging down and allow it to dangle.
   Raise your upperbody by rolling up vertebra after vertebra until
   the head arrives last in the height and the spine is straight.
   Let your upperbody sink, dangle to the right side and rise, then let
   it sink, dangle to the left side and rise. Give in at the knees by
   bending them slightly. This is not a side-bend but a collapse of the
   spine to the side. Make sure again that the head is last to roll up.
   Let the upperbody sink diagonally forward over the right leg and
   rise, then let it sink diagonally forward over the left leg and rise.
   Let the neck, head, shoulders and arms sink diagonally back in the
   direction of the right heel and rise, and then sink diagonally back
   in the direction of the left heel and rise.
   When you sink diagonally back do not curve in the centre of the
   spine. Drop the jaw and leave the throat open. Always check on
   breathing out when you sink and breathing in when you rise.

2. Let the upperbody sink forward and fall between the legs as
   before. Bend the knees as much as to make it comfortable to put
   the palms of your hands on the floor.
   Push with your hands a small distance away from the floor and
   drop then back again. The upperbody still hangs loosely from the
   base of the spine and the hand-push does not raise the level of the
   trunk. The vertebrae should respond to the hand-push with waves
   going through the whole of the spine.
   Rise without lifting but roll the spine slowly up again until it
   stretches to the upright. Always leave the higher part passive until
   its weight is lifted by the part below it, and wait for the weight of
   the head to be rolled up and lightly poised on top of the spine.
   Check on placement of the pelvis, centre, shoulders, neck and
   head.

Hips, Legs and Feet

1. Stand with the feet together. Pull the right upperleg into the socket of its joint and lift the right hip. This is a similar movement to pulling up the shoulder-balls. As you pull the leg up it is lifted slightly off the floor and feels shorter than the other leg.
Leave the leg absolutely passive and let it dangle.
Let it sink and feel it lengthening out of its joint. Do the same with the left leg and hip.

The legs fall straight under and are neither turned inwards nor outwards in the hip-joints.

2. Raise one leg forward without pulling it into the socket of the hip-joint. Leave the leg on 'long strings'.
Let the leg sink.
Raise the leg to the side and let it sink.
Raise the leg to the back and let it sink. Repeat with the other leg.

When you raise the legs remain still and upright with the upperbody. When you let the legs sink shake the knees out gently and let the muscles of the legs vibrate.

3. Lift one foot very slightly off the floor in front. Let the foot hang very loosely and shake it from the ankle on a count of eight.
Change to the other foot.

Make sure you work only with the parts which are engaged in loosening out and check that spine, shoulders, arms and hands remain relaxed.

Knees

When you stand the knees point in the direction of the toes. If you turn your knees inward the thighs pull close, the legs twist and the arches of the feet incline to drop. If you strain the knees outward or overstretch them you cause tensions and incline to lift the pelvis. Naturally in the experience of movement you go very far from the centre and in the practice of movement you might go to extremes of stretch and bend and of in- and out-turns, but above and below, inward and outward are related to a middle from where they are controlled.

In a kneebend the balance is very easily upset by tensions in the spine and by pulling shoulders and arms. If you have difficulties in a kneebend realize that balance IS good placement. When you push, press or pull one part of the spine in or out, or up, or to the side, you upset the balance. Most of the work in a kneebend is done by the leg-muscles. Muscles strengthen through practice but they are greatly assisted by the placement of structure and weight. The spine does not help you to lift and it does not assist you when you lower into or rise from a kneebend. Therefore you practise kneebends first with a collapse of the vertebral column. This enables you to leave the spine disengaged, relaxed and straight when you work on kneebends which demand perfect balance.

1. Stand with your feet about 18 inches apart. Drop the pelvis and bend your knees. Round the tail-end of the spine to the middle between your legs.
   Drop into a kneebend as low as you can and let the spine collapse forward. Round the back and tuck the tail well in. Keep the soles of the feet on the floor.
   Do not stay in the kneebend but try to use the rebound of the fall of weight to help you to straighten the legs up again. As they straighten roll up the spine until you stand upright.
   Do the same with your feet standing closer and also with a closed foot-position when the heels will lift. Try to lower the seat towards the heels and if you can, round it under the heels.
   Do the same in a step-position. The sole of the foot in front is on the floor and the heel of the foot at the back is lifted. Your weight lowers in the middle.
   You might fall when going up or down. You should always be ready to drop your head and round your back forward, and touch the floor with the soft parts of your seat (and not with the pointed end of the spine) but with the tail well tucked in.

2. Stand with your feet about 24 inches apart and drop into a knee-bend, as you did in the first exercise of this sequence, but this time stay down. Round the seat into the middle between your legs as much as you can.
   Lower the seat slowly, and if it touches or very nearly touches the floor, sit down. Do not let the upperbody fall back but round it over the legs.
   Unroll the spine slowly until the whole of your back lies flat. Lift the legs, shake the knees and feet and loosen them well out.

The Whole Body

Stand and lift your arms and stretch yourself upwards with a big yawn going through your body.

As you release the stretch sigh out and collapse very slowly on to the floor. Do not throw yourself or throw any weight away from you, but let the weight bit by bit sink under within your body. Curl inwardly and round yourself outwardly.

Let your body roll and then spread on the floor. Spread as if melting. As you sprawl on the floor make sure every bit of you (this naturally includes the jaw, tongue, eyes, etc.) is equally and totally passive.

At this point it is helpful to have a partner — 'a counterplayer' to whom you say 'do with me what you like,' and whom you permit to touch you and move you, roll, drag, and lift you while you remain passively non-resisting. There are many themes which can be based on this exercise. For instance, Cain's attempt to bring Abel back to life or a child's attempt to repair a broken doll.

Coil and Uncoil the Whole Body

Stand in a step-position with the left foot forward. The soles of both feet are on the floor and the weight-line drops in the middle between the feet. Raise the right arm upward and stretch yourself from feet to fingertips and breathe in.

Coil in with the right hand and arm rounding over your head and coil in with the whole of the spine. Bend the knees and tuck the tail in.

Sink into a deep kneebend, lower the seat to the ground and sit down. Remain with the upperbody rounded over the right thigh and knee.

Uncoil the upperbody on to the floor and stretch out.

Bend the right leg and coil the upperbody up again to the right thigh and knee. Try to get up into a one-legged kneebend without pausing. If you fail to do this, press with the left hand on the floor and assist the seat to lift off the floor.

Bend the left knee and put the sole of the foot on the floor. Retrace your way up. Uncoil until you finish as you started. Do the same again with the right foot forward and the left arm raised. You realize this coiling and uncoiling or folding and unfolding even more if you accompany the movement with a half-turn. A step-position has a closed and an open side for turning. The legs close and cross if you turn to the side of the foot in front. The legs open and allow you to turn quite easily to the side of the foot at the back.

Coil and turn to the open side on the down-movement and uncoil and retrace the turn on the up-movement. Vocalize a count of twelve on the down-movement. Breathe in when you stretch on the floor and vocalize a count of twelve on the up-movement. Do the movement twice very slowly, twice faster and twice very fast. Practise it with fluency and in the right order. Think of an elastic string which coils and uncoils.

Fall and Rebound

Stand with your feet slightly apart. Jump and as you touch ground rebound from the fall of weight. Feel the soles of your feet push away from the floor. As you bounce remain 'all in one', that is, quite still but relaxed. Make sure the shoulders do not move. They have a habit of going up and down which does not help the bounce.
Bounce and shake the arms, hands, legs and feet away from you into the air. Give a short shout as you bounce.
Repeat the bounce and as the feet touch ground, collapse and sink on to the floor.
Get up at once, bounce immediately again and stand.

From Kneebend to Sitting

Coiling and Uncoiling
From Horizontal to Vertical and Reverse

Sinking

Sprawling   Spreading

35

4 TUNING AND RESILIENCE

Loose or tight strings produce dud-sounds. Loose or tight muscles produce dud-movements. If you are too loosely strung you fall to the ground and cannot get up. If you are too tightly strung you are cramped and cannot move at all or you move and something snaps and you hurt yourself. You are well strung or tuned when all parts are in their rightful places, and ligaments, tendons and muscles have their full length, strength and elasticity.

The next movements use the impetus of the free fall into gravity by directing it into *The Swing.* The swinging movement develops the smallest vibration of to-ing and fro-ing into distances from near to far, and from low to high, and into circles and curves.

There is a vibration within your body which is unnoticeable from the outside. This vibration is the beginning of the swing which only stops when you stop breathing. Naturally you have the power to enlarge, to diminish or to bring the swing outwardly to a halt.

The practice of the swinging movements links the centre with the periphery, binds below and above to each other and relates heaviness to lightness. By doing so, it furthers the resilience of the body and enlarges the movability of the joints.

If you lift one arm forward and drop it freely without holding its weight, it swings backwards and forwards. It continues this motion of a pendulum as long as you drop it freely from the height to which the swing carries it. After the initial lifting of the arm you do not have to lift it again. The arm is carried upward by the swing without effort. The size and length of the swing are maintained by the impetus of the free fall. The phrase of the swinging movement is heavy and quick in the beginning, lighter and slower in the middle and very light and very slow towards its end until it dies out. When given time to move itself out the swing changes direction and falls back. Its very end is the beginning of the next swing.

There are five points to watch when you practise these movements:

a   to let the weight fall freely and catch the rebound
b   to breathe out on the down-movement and breathe in on and at the very end of the up-movement
c   to remain relaxed
d   to enlarge the swing by the impetus of the fall of weight and not by lifting
e   to leave the swing time to move out to its end and wait until it changes direction

PRACTICE

Neck

Pendulum swing
Drop the head forward with its entire weight and swing it from
side to side.
Enlarge the swing until the neck stretches towards the centre.

Circular swing
Roll the head round: drop it to the right, swing it over the front
to the left, roll it over the back to the right, drop it in front,
swing it out on the left, then reverse the direction of the rotation.

Curved swing
Stretch your neck well in the centre. Drop the head, swing it to
the right and curve it up with a circular movement over the right
shoulder.
As you return to the centre drop the head again, swing it to the
left and curve it up with a circular movement over the left
shoulder. The two adjacent circles form the figure of a horizontal
EIGHT. The head does not tilt back. When you swing out the
neck-muscles stretch straight from the back and the head moves
over the height.

Arms

The arms help to clarify the directions but it is really the shoulders
which matter. Movement compares with sound which follows after
the touch of the key on the keyboard. Your arms move in consequence
of your touching the shoulder-joints.

Pendulum swing
Stand in a step-position and lift one arm in front and the other to
the back up to shoulder-height.
Drop the arms and swing them freely backwards and forwards.
The length and height of the swing should be equal in front and at
the back.
Enlarge the impetus of the fall to carry the arms higher. To achieve
height the arm at the back has to turn in the socket of the shoulder-
joint.

Circular swing
Stand in a step-position with the right foot forward and lift the left arm at the back.
Drop the left arm down, swing it to the front, fling it over the height to the back, drop it, let it swing out to the front and reverse the direction. Change to the other arm.
As the arms swing say to yourself:
FORE/UP — back/down and fore — BACK/UP — fore/down and back.
Allow the movement to slow down over the height and make sure not to curve in the centre of the spine, or pull on chest, neck or jaw. Do not force the size of the circles. They will enlarge gradually.

Lasso swing
Stand with the feet apart and lift one arm to the side to shoulder-height. Swing the arm over your head by moving it first towards you, then well to the back and then allow it time to straighten out to the side before you swing again. The palm of the hand is turned downward in the beginning and turned upward at the end of the movement. Do this eight times slowly and eight times quickly to a count of one, two, THREE. Then let the arm drop and dangle. Feel it to be completely free-hanging and change to the other arm.

Shoulder-Balls

Circular swing
Stand with the feet slightly apart and roll the shoulder-balls.
Raise the shoulder-balls, drop them forward, swing them up and let them drop to the back and swing out to the front. Then reverse the direction of the rotation. As the shoulder-balls swing, say to yourself: FORE/UP — back/down and FORE
BACK/UP — fore/down and BACK

Elbows

Circular swing
Raise the arms to the side to shoulder-height. The palms of the hands are turned downward. Keep the upper-arms up and as still as possible. Drop the lower-arms from the elbows and circle with them eight times towards you and eight times away from you. Drop the arms.

Hands

Circular swing

Raise the arms again to the side and keep them still. Drop the hands from the wrists and circle with them eight times starting to the front and eight times starting to the back. Drop the arms.

Curved swing

Raise the arms in front of you. Drop the hands towards you and curve them up and drop them away from you and curve them up. Do this eight times and drop the arms. This swing forms two adjacent circles of the figure of a horizontal EIGHT. As the hands move say to yourself: in/up and out/up.

Upperbody

Pendulum swing

Stand in a step-position and lift the arms upward. Bend the straight upperbody forward until it is in a right angle to the legs. Feel the tension caused by holding the straight spine in this position. Bend the knees a little.

Let the upperbody fall heavily from the centre of the spine and swing it towards and away from the legs. The arms follow the fall of the upperbody and swing backwards and forwards. Do not lift the upperbody. The swing raises the spine only as far as the right angle-bend from where it started. The swings should be of equal length and they should round and straighten the spine as follows:

a round — as the trunk falls
b straight — as the spine swings out and away when the arms are at the back
c round — as the trunk falls again
d straight — as the spine swings out and away again when the arms are in front

Make sure that the head falls with its entire weight towards the legs on the down-movement and the neck stretches well on the away-movement. As you swing with the upperbody say to yourself: down/round and straight/back . . . . . down/round and straight/front.

Down and Up swing

Stand with your feet together and lift the arms upward. Let the upperbody fall heavily down and swing it to the legs. The arms continue to swing out to the back at the sides of your legs. Catch the rebound of the fall of the upperbody and let it unroll the spine until it arrives in the height. This movement does not touch the bend of the upperbody in the right angle to the legs. The spine is carried upwards until it straightens. This is an uneven swing. The down-fall is fast and the upward-movement gets gradually slower until it swings out on the top. There you sway a little, feel for lightness and breathe in. Breathe out when you let the upperbody fall again and join your breath to sound.

Diagonal swing

This swing moves from side to side but does not bend the upper-body to the side.

Stand with your feet about 16 inches apart. Plant the feet very firmly on the ground. They should not shift or move about when you swing with the upperbody. Grip the floor with the toes. Make sure the pelvis is dropped. Raise the arms upward and incline with the upperbody and the arms to the right.

Let the upperbody fall over the right leg, down between both legs and swing up over the left leg. The impetus of the fall should carry the trunk up to the diagonal on the left from where it falls again and swings to the other side. The arms must not swing separately. Remain 'all in one' from the base of the spine to the fingertips.

Side swing

In this movement you direct the upperbody to turn from the diagonal to the side.

Start as before. As you swing over the left leg roll the upperbody over the hip and stretch it well out to the left side. The head and chest face to the front and the arms remain at the sides of the head.

Let the upperbody topple over the hip, drop forward and down, swing to the right, roll over the hip and stretch out to the right side.

Circular swing
Stand as before with the feet apart and firmly planted on the
floor. Swing once to each side and with the momentum gained roll
the upperbody round.
Swing to the right and swing to the left. Count: one and two.
Swing to the right, back, left, down and right.
Count: one, two, three, four and five.
Repeat the swing starting to the left.
Let the upperbody fall freely forward into depth. At the back drop
the head and shoulders gently and do not bend low from the
centre of the spine. Enlarge the circles gradually and swing well
out to the sides.

Wheel swing
Stand in a step-position with the left foot forward and raise the
right arm at the back. Let the upperbody and arm fall forward
and swing up.
Fling over the height, drop gently back and let the arm swing out
to the front.
Let the upperbody fall a little at the back and swing up.
Fling over the height, drop forward and let the arm swing out to
the back.
The swing moves like a wheel which rolls backwards and forwards.
As the wheel gets gradually bigger allow it more time to move
over the height. As you swing say to yourself:
FORE/UP — back/fore . . . and BACK/UP — fore/back . . .

Lasso swing
Stand very firmly with the feet apart and lift the right arm to the
side to shoulder-height.
Swing the arm towards you and swing the upperbody over the
front to the left and over the back to the right. Let the swing slow
down in front and die out on the left and pause.
Swing the right arm from the left away from you to the right and
swing the upperbody to the right and over the back to the left. Let
the swing slow down in front and die out on the right and pause.
Start this swing quickly and let it slow down gradually until both
it and you come to rest. You should feel as if a strong gust whirls
your upperbody round to one side, leaves it to rest for a moment
and whirls it round to the other side. Breathe in before you start
to swing and let the breath go with the swing on the sounds of:
Tataataaataaaataaaaataaaaaataaaaaaata
1 2 3 4   5   6   7   8

Pelvis

Circular swings to the front and to the back
  Stand with the feet together. Lift one hip and pull the leg up into the socket of the hip-joint. Leave the leg hanging freely.
  Drop the hip and the leg and roll:
  down/fore/up/back/down/fore and up,
  down/back/up/fore/down/back and up. Let the hip and leg drop straight down and change to the other hip and leg.
  Stand with the feet slightly apart and bend the knees a little. Lift the pelvis, drop it and roll:
  down/fore/up/back/down/fore and up,
  down/back/up/fore/down/back and up. Lower the pelvis well down.

Circular swing to the sides
  Stand as before. Lift the pelvis and drop it and roll:
  down/right/up/left/down and up,
  down/left/up/right/down and up. Lower the pelvis well down again in the centre.

Legs

The following sequence of movements requires you to stand on one leg but they are not balance-exercises. If you have difficulties in standing on one leg hold on lightly with one hand on the back of a chair. The point of practising these movements is to enlarge the freedom and movability of the legs in the hip-joints. Balance is based on body-placement. If you raise one leg, the centre of your weight or your weight-line must transfer to the other leg. The leg which is in the air must leave the rest of the body disengaged and move freely in the socket of its joint. It upsets the balance when it pulls other parts out of place.
Start by transferring your weight-line over one leg. Lift the leg which does not support any weight. Raise the arms to the sides to form a horizontal cross-beam to your perpendicular centre-structure and look at a fixed point at eye-level straight in front of you.

Pendulum swing

Raise one leg in front and bend the knee slightly.

Let the thigh fall heavily and swing the leg out to the back. Do not hold the leg or cut the swing short but wait until it changes its direction.

Let the thigh fall and swing the leg out in front. Leave the leg-muscles as relaxed as possible. After the initial raising of the leg you do not have to lift it again. The impetus of the fall of the thigh should continue the movement and should carry the leg upwards. As the leg swings say to yourself: back/up and fore/up. After eight swings change to the other leg.

Side swing

Turn the right leg inward in the socket of its joint and raise it. The knee points to the other leg and the lower leg moves to the right side.

Let the thigh fall and swing the leg across over the front to the left and away to the right. It is still turned inward.

When the leg arrives at the height on the right side, turn it outward in the socket of its joint, let the swing die out and straighten the knee. Then let the leg gently drop to the floor. As the leg swings say to yourself: in/in and OUT. Lengthen the leg out when the hip opens. Practise the movement eight times with each leg. It must make you feel the closing and opening of the hip and the upper-leg turning in its joint. Think of a key which turns in the keyhole to one side and closes the lock and turns to the other side and opens it.

Curved swing

Turn one leg inwards and raise it.

Let the thigh fall and swing the leg across over the front, curve up to the out-side and open the hip.

Let the thigh fall and swing back, curve up to the side and leave the hip open. Then let the thigh fall again from an inward-turned leg. The swing moves in the shape of a horizontal figure of EIGHT which curves in the front and at the back of you. As the leg swings say to yourself: in/up and out/up. Practise the movement eight times with each leg. It should make the hip-joints feel well 'oiled'. It is good to increase and decrease the tempi of the swinging movements. The impetus of the fall of the thighs carries the legs higher when you swing fast. When you swing slowly the legs gain in elastic length and sustaining power.

Feet

Circular swing

Sit on the floor and lift the right leg. Hold the leg with your hands under the thigh. Bend the knee and let the lower leg and the foot hang freely.

Lift the foot and drop it and let it roll round starting once to the left and once to the right. Say to yourself:

down/left/up/right/down/up and down/right/up/left/down/up.

After eight circular movements shake the foot and change to the other foot.

Curved swing

Start from the same position as before and lift the foot.

Drop the foot and swing it inwards, curving up in the centre.

Drop the foot again and swing it outwards, curving up in the centre. After eight swings shake the foot out and change to the other foot. The swing joins two adjacent circles in the form of a horizontal figure of EIGHT.

The swinging movements lubricate the joints and prepare the elastic extension of the connective tissues, ligaments and muscles. They do not sustain length or breadth. Their outgoing motion retracts as soon as it has arrived at the distance effected by the fall of weight.

You must let the swing work for you. After the initial lift and after the first fall of weight, the swing should continue the movement by the impetus of the fall without your effort. The swing should move you and stretch the elasticity of your body without you exerting yourself. By your inaction you are being moved by the swing. In the next chapter the movements are activated by YOU.

Pendulum Swing

Side-Swing

47

Wheel-Swing

48

Curved Swing

5   *LENGTH AND BREADTH*

Physical activity must not and need not disturb your being when
engaged in acting.

Imagine you are called upon to fall quickly on your knees,
simultaneously stretch the upperbody and arms to the height and
sing out with your whole voice. The fall on the knees causes a
momentary pain which registers in your face, shoulders and voice and
the spectator's attention is distracted from the dramatic action.

The skeletal muscles of the lower limbs, linked with the mobility of
the pelvis, feet and knees, support and free the upperbody for you to
choose to move it or not to move it and to use voice as much as you
will. The skeletal muscles shield the internal muscles and you must
be able to rely on the length and breadth of the skeletal muscles to
support and sustain your movements.

When the body closes it turns to the inside and bends. When it opens
it turns to the outside and stretches. Inner and outer are bound to
each other. You collect inwardly in order to reach out and share out.
The following sequence of movements should be worked with particular care and intensity. Employ only those parts and muscle-groups
which are necessary for specific movement to be effective and leave
the rest of the body disengaged.

PRACTICE

Feet

1. Sit on the floor and lift one foot.
   Bend the foot upwards.
   Bend the toes down. Leave the rest of the foot up.
   Stretch the instep.
   Bend the toes up. Leave the instep stretched.
   Bend the whole foot up.
Say to yourself: toes/down-foot/down-toes/up-foot/up. After eight
times shake the foot out and change to the other foot.

2. Stand with the feet together. Set one foot at a right angle to the
   other and bend the knee a little. Lift the toes and the ball of the
   foot so that only the heel touches the floor.
   Crawl with the foot from heel to ball to toe away to the side. Lift
   the stretched foot slightly off the floor and start again from the
   heel. Do this three times, return the foot and set it down on its
   entire sole in the starting position.
Say to yourself: heel/ball/toe/—heel/ball/toe/—heel/ball/toe and back.
After eight times change to the other foot.

3. Stand with your feet about 24 inches apart. Bend the knees a little
   and lift the heel of one foot as high as you can.
   Put this heel down, lift the other heel and put it down.
   Lift both heels and put them down and start with one heel again.
Say to yourself: up/down, up/down and both up/down. Do this only
four times and loosen the legs and feet out.

4. Stand with your feet together and lift the heels.
   Lower the heels on to the floor, give a little at the knees and jump.
   Push the weight away from the floor in the order of: heel, ball,
   toe. Straighten the legs and feet in the air and land the weight on
   the floor in the order of: toe, ball, heel and give a little at the
   knees.
   Stand with the feet apart and do the same.
   Stand with the feet together, jump again and pull the thighs up
   bending the knees in the air.
While engaging the feet- calf and thigh-muscles check on the upperbody to remain upright, still and free.

Kneebend, Kneeling and Sitting

1. Stand with your feet slightly apart and raise your arms forward to shoulder-level. Bend the knees a little and move the pelvis forwards and backwards.

2. Do the same with the upperbody bending forward when the pelvis moves back and with the upperbody leaning backwards when the pelvis moves forward.

Engage the thigh- and pelvis-muscles when the upperbody leans back and form a diagonal line from knees to head.

3. Stand with your feet together and lower into a deep kneebend. Leave your heels as long as possible on the floor and check that the knees point in the direction of the toes. Make sure that the seat lowers under the spine with a well tucked-in tail-end and the upperbody remains free and upright.
   Raise by engaging the thigh-muscles, lower the heels on to the floor as soon as possible and straighten the legs. Feel for the spine, shoulders and head to be free.

Bend to a count of four and rise to a count of five or speak any text in the rhythm of the count.

4. Stand in a step-position with the right foot forward and lower into a deep kneebend. Grip the floor with the whole of the right foot in front and lift the heel of the left foot at the back.
   Pause in the kneebend and make sure that the spine is upright and disengaged and the face is relaxed.
   Rise and straighten the legs slowly. Change to the left foot forward.

Bend to a count of two and pause. Rise to a count of five or speak any text while you move and while you pause.

5. Stand with the feet about 16 inches apart. Lift the left heel and
   turn the left thigh and knee inward.
   Bend the knees slowly and lower the left knee gently to the floor.
   Leave the right thigh turned outward, the knee off the floor and
   the foot on the floor.
   Now lift the right heel and turn the right thigh and knee inward.
   Lower the right knee gently to the floor next to the left knee.
   Lift the left knee and turn the thigh outward. Put the heel on the
   floor.
   Lift the right knee and turn the thigh outward. Put the heel on the
   floor. Open both thighs from the hips.
   Rise slowly and straighten the legs. Repeat starting with the other
   leg.
Engage the thigh- and pelvis-muscles and rely on them to support you
when you lower into and rise from the kneebend. Make sure the
spine remains upright and straight and you are facing to the front all
the time. Say to yourself: in and in-out and OUT and count five on
rising. Practise this movement only four to six times and then loosen
the legs and feet out.

6. Take a stool and sit on it. Put one foot slightly in front of the
   other. Make sure the spine is upright and free.
   Rise without bending forward. Engage the thigh-muscles, straighten
   the legs and keep the spine disengaged.
   Sit down again without bending forward. Bend the knees, lower the
   pelvis, tuck the tail-end in and keep the spine disengaged.
Do this slowly at first. Gradually increase the tempo and join your
breathing to sounds or speak.

7. Kneel down with the knees close to each other and lower the seat
   until it touches the heels.
   Move the pelvis forward until you form a diagonal line from knees
   to head and lower the seat again to the heels.
   Repeat the movement turning the upperbody to the right and left.
   Do the same with the knees apart.
Practise the sequence of these three movements only three or four
times and then sit down and loosen the legs and feet out.
In the following two movements the knees are lowered very gently
until they touch the floor and must not crash down.

8. Stand with the feet together, bend the knees a little and move the pelvis forward.

Keep the pelvis forward and continue to lower the knees until they reach the floor.

Lift one knee, place the foot firmly on the floor and rise in a step-position. Straighten the legs, close the feet and repeat.

Do the same standing with the feet about 16 inches apart and lower the knees slowly to the floor.

Lift one knee, open the thigh and put the heel down, then lift the other knee, open the thigh and put the heel down.

Grip the floor firmly and straighten the legs.

Practise these movements only two to four times. Rely on the skeletal muscles of the lower limbs, feel for their support and make sure the upper-body remains free. Speak as you move and check whether breath and voice work quite unhindered.

The next two movements make considerable demands on the thigh-muscles. Practise them when you are sure you can rely on the thigh-muscles to give you the necessary support. In case these muscles 'let you down' in the course of any of the movements, drop the head down, roll the spine quickly forward and tuck the tail-end well in. By doing so you either land with the seat on the floor or you flop into a kneebend.

9. Sit on the floor and bend your knees. Move the feet as near as possible to your seat and put the palms of your hands at the sides of your seat with the fingers pointing forward.

Move the pelvis upward and stretch the thighs forward until the knees touch the floor.

Lift your hands off the floor and move the upperbody forward until it and the thighs are at a right angle to the lower legs.

Lower the seat, round the spine putting your hands back on the floor and lift your knees. Return to the starting position.

Practise this slowly at first and gradually increase the tempo.

10. Stand with the feet about 18 inches apart and lower into a deep kneebend opening the thighs.

Tuck the tail-end in as much as possible, lower the seat between the legs as far down as you can and put your hands on the floor. Touch the floor gently with the well rounded-in seat and sit.

Move the seat up and engage the thigh-muscles to lift you.

Take the hands off the floor and roll the spine up until you stand up straight. Make sure the upperbody, shoulders, jaw and throat remain free.

Practise the next two movements with the hands touching the floor at first. When you can rely entirely on thighs and knees move without the help of your hands.

11. Stand with the feet together and let the whole of your weight sway
   forward without bending the body.
   At the moment the weight over-balances, move one foot forward
   and land in a big stride.
   Lower the knee in front to the floor and sink with the upperbody
   slowly to the ground. This movement should give you the feeling
   of gliding forward and landing smoothly.
   Move the leg from the back to the front and put the foot down.
   Round the spine over the knee.
   Straighten up into a step-position. Close the feet and start again,
   moving the other leg forward as you do so.
Breathe in on rising and standing. Breathe out, sigh out or sing out
on gliding forward to the floor.

12. Stand with the feet together and let the whole of your weight
   sway to the left side.
   At the moment the weight over-balances move the right leg across
   the left, bend the knees and, keeping the right foot on the floor,
   glide slowly to the side on to the ground.
   Rise by slowly rounding the spine over the right thigh. Straighten
   the legs while rolling the upperbody upward and close the feet.
   Repeat, changing over to the other side. Sigh out or sing out when
   gliding to the floor.

Shoulder-balls, Shoulder-blades and Rib-cage

Practise the following movements for the extension of the movability of the arms and the expansion of the rib-cage. The rib-cage or thorax expands and contracts and allows inflation and deflation of the lungs. In the back the ribs have tiny gliding and rotating joints which enable them to articulate with the spine. When the shoulder-balls roll in and turn out the shoulder-blades open and close. Breathe out on rolling in and breathe in on rolling out. Keep checking that the neck and jaw are free and are not pulled by the shoulder- and arm-movements. When the shoulder-balls roll in bend the elbows slightly and curl the fingers in. When the shoulder-balls turn out make sure they and the shoulder-blades drop. Stretch the elbows and fingers and lengthen the arm well out.

1. Stand with the feet apart, raise the left arm to shoulder-level, roll the shoulder-ball in and drop the head to the left.
   Roll the shoulder-ball out, turning the head to the right and straighten the neck.
   Say to yourself: in and OUT, in and OUT.
   Do the same movement and enlarge it by stretching the out-rolling arm backwards. Loosen the arm and neck out and change to the other arm.
   Raise both arms to the sides to shoulder-level and roll the left shoulder-ball in and turn the right shoulder-ball out.
   Interchange by rolling the right shoulder-ball in and turning the left shoulder-ball out.
   Say to yourself: in/out, in/out.
   Do the same movement and enlarge it by stretching the out-rolling arms backwards and say: in/OUT, in/OUT.
   Loosen both arms and neck out.
   While practising these movements keep checking that the spine and chest remain in the centre.

2. Stand in a step-position with the right foot forward and move the left arm back to shoulder-level. Roll the shoulder-ball in, bend the elbow slightly, curl the fingers in and drop the head forward.
   Turn the shoulder-ball out and lengthen the arm behind you straightening the neck, elbow and fingers. Make sure the spine and chest remain in the centre.
   Drop the head forward and roll the arm in. Say to yourself: in and OUT, and in and OUT.
   Shake the arm out and change to the other arm at the back and the other foot in front.
   Do the same movement and enlarge it by raising the arm upward from the back. Say to yourself: in/OUT/up and back, in/OUT/up and back.

Stand with the feet apart and do the same with both arms without curving the centre of the spine inwards. Think of the span and beat of wings. Loosen the shoulders, arms and hands well out by shaking them.

Hands

1. Sit on the floor, raise your arms forward to shoulder-level, bend the elbows and turn the palms of the hands towards you.
Bend the fingers and make fists.
Straighten the knuckles of the hands, slowly stretch the fingers, spread them and make fists again.
Do this to a count of one, two, three, four, FIVE and after moving the hands in this way four to six times shake them well out.

2. Raise the arms to the sides, bend the hands downwards from the wrists and make fists.
Lift the hands upwards, straighten the knuckles, slowly stretch the fingers, lengthen them out and spread them wide.
Slowly curl the fingers under, move the hands down and make fists again. Do this eight times on a count of seven. After moving the hands with intensity and fluency loosen them well out by shaking them.

Face

Think of making a fist with your face, close it tight, 'screw it up', very slowly open it bit by bit and leave it open and still.

Eyes

Close and open your eyes engaging only the eyelids.
Focus near and far.
Movements which are inward-turning or folding and outward-turning or unfolding, narrow and widen in equal measure. On opening they reach out and emanate in space and their power of penetration is not in their size but in their concentration.

Pelvis fore and back

Pelvis back/Upperbody fore/Pelvis fore/Upperbody back

Inwards turned Kneeling/Outwards turned Rising

Open Kneeling and Rising

From Sitting to Kneeling

Pelvis and thighs forward into diagonal line from knees to head

Fall forward

Fall to the side

6 CONFLUENCE

It is quite natural for you to go or run from A to B or to talk and
walk simultaneously. You also possess the superfluidity of energy to
skip over flagstones, which is so natural to the child. Your walk glides
into dancing and your voice overflows into singing without practice.
On the sophisticated level of preparing a performance, it is the usual
practice to divide the rehearsing of text from 'placing', 'moves' and
'movement' first and to put it all together when nearing the first
night. Performing in front of an audience demands the transformation
of NATURE into ART and necessitates inquiry and information. Such
simple and natural physical activities as walking and running become
complicated when taken apart. You go through considerable complexities in order to arrive at a second simplicity.
The confluence of movement and sound springs from the same source.
You walk and talk with the same breath and it is good practice to
join movement to breath-sound, to speaking and singing. You can
use sounds like bubbling, burbling, buzzing, humming, la-la-ing,
ta-ta-ing and can speak or sing rhythmical and melodious phrases
while you move.
If you observe the walk of four-legged animals, and particularly of
those of the cat-family, you will notice how the thrust of the limbs
starts from the vertebral column and consequently moves to the
pelvis, shoulder-blades and legs. The spine reacts to every foot-fall.
Step, spine, neck and head synchronize.
Man moves in a similar fashion, as Leonardo da Vinci observed:
'The walking of men is always after the universal walking of animals
with four legs inasmuch as just as they move their feet crosswise after
the manner of the trot of the horse, so man moves his four limbs
crosswise; that is if he puts forward his right foot in walking he with
it puts forward his left arm, and vice versa, invariably.'
The path in space and the path in time is often condensed on stage.
The spectator must be convinced that the actor covers bigger and
longer distances than he actually travels. Therefore using a confined
space which merely allows you to walk, run, jump, or turn only on
the spot, to and fro and around, is useful practice and will test your
freedom and control of movement within limitations.

There are as many variations of walking as there are variations of character. The following sequence of movements invites you to practise variations on the theme of walking. It also invites to caricature but the importance of the movements is the experience of the effect of physical changes on walk and voice. Speak any text you know well while you walk and feel for and take note of the change of voice with the change in the manner of walking.

After a few steps in a particular manner of walking resume and continue with your own way of walking. As there are countless variations make your own additions to the list.

Walk: a stiffening the spine and feel how one step separates from the other
b pulling the neck forward
c lifting the chin up
d dropping the head forward
e lifting the shoulders up
f pulling the shoulders back
g dropping the shoulders forward
h holding the arms stiff
i moving the arms from the elbows
j turning the hips, knees and toes inward
k turning the hips, knees and toes outward
l bouncing from foot to foot
m shuffling with the feet
n bending the feet upwards and letting the weight fall on the heels
o dropping the weight from side to side and note how this tilts and shifts the pelvis
p bending the upperbody forward and note the heavy fall of weight
q swaying with the upperbody
r leaning with the whole body backwards and note how this leaves the weight behind you as you walk forward.

PRACTICE

Walking

1. Position yourself on hands and knees, curve the spine and lift the left leg up at the back.
   Round the spine and move the left leg forward to your head. Lower the left knee to the floor, stretch the spine and move the right arm forward. Curve the spine, lift the right leg back and continue with the sequence.
   Enlarge the walk on all fours by
   a lengthening and lowering the body further to the floor and
   b by rounding the spine more, swinging the arms and lifting the knees off the floor.

2. Stand in a step-position, put the palms of your hands on your back and lightly touch with your fingers in the centre of the spine.
   Walk and feel for a very fine feathering movement in the centre of your spine. This movement should not be noticeable from the outside but there is a very slight action and reaction in the centre of the spine and every step begins and ends in the centre.
   Start the following sequence of movements in slow motion and gradually increase the tempo to normal speed, always making sure that the shoulders, arms, legs, hands and feet are free, the neck is straightened from the back and the spine is relaxed.

3. Begin from a step-position, with the right leg forward, the left leg back, the arms slightly raised in opposite directions to the legs and your weight in front over the right foot.
   Move the left leg forward, touching the floor lightly, and transfer the weight on to the left foot at the same time and in equal measure as you release it from the right foot. When the weight has rolled over the entire sole of the left foot move the right leg forward and continue. The arms should swing slightly in the opposite direction to the legs.
   Walking without motivation is unnatural. After walking through the sequence several times, give yourself a simple motive, such as, 'I have to go and open the window'. By frequent practice the movements synchronize as you stop thinking about them and they become natural.
   Walk forward, backwards and around. Vocalize your breathing or speak while you walk. When you walk forward give way to the tendency of the weight to lean very slightly to the front. When you walk backwards give way to the tendency of the weight to lean very slightly back and lessen the arm- and leg-swing. When you walk around give way to the tendency of the weight to lean very slightly into the circle or curve.

Run

Stand and breathe in. As you begin to breathe out run forward
singing out on 'haaaaaaaa' for as long as your outgoing breath lasts.
Then turn on the spot, breathe in and repeat.
Movement and sound form a synchronized phrase. Think of a
curve in the air.
Run backwards on breathing out rounding the upperbody forward.
Run backwards on breathing out stretching the upperbody.
Feel for the air at the back of you and rely on it to support and
cushion you like water does for the swimmer.

Jump

Enlarge the run into jumping. Feel how the rebound from weight
lifts you. Swing the legs more freely and jump higher. Keep the
body still but not stiff and let the feet do the work. The feet take
off from the floor in succession of heel, ball, toe and land in succession of toe, ball, heel.

Turn

Stand in a step-position with the right foot in front. Raise the left
arm at the back to shoulder-level and roll the shoulder-ball
inwards.
Turn the shoulder-ball outwards and let the body follow the arm-
movement into a half-turn. Change to the left foot in front and the
right arm at the back.
Lift the left leg up backwards and roll it inwards in the hip-joint.
Roll it outwards and let the body follow the leg-movement into a
half-turn. Step on to the left foot and do the same with the right
leg.
Step on the ball of the left foot and raise the heel as high as you
can. Bring the heel forward as you lower it to the floor and let the
body follow the outward movement of the foot, knee and thigh
into a quarter-turn to the left. Step out with the right foot and do
the same.
Stand with the feet apart, jump and turn. Now stand with the feet
together, jump and turn. Enlarge the turns gradually from quarter-
to half- to full-turns.
Kneel and lean with the upperbody backwards.
Turn over to the side and rise.

Kinetic energy and kinetic memory must both work for you in
rehearsal and performance. Movements flow gently, beat boldly — cut
sharply. Their rhythms and melodies dictate precision of timing and

spacing. Physical action must not halt dramatic action and must not call attention to itself. Skills such as tumbling, acrobatics, fencing, juggling and dancing only enrich the theatre if the actor can act through them. Stand and walk on your hands, act and speak a line by Shakespeare, if the character and situation call for this, and if you are able to do it without breaking the dramatic continuity. Practise for continuity, for crescendos and decrescendos and for control of the potent pause which holds the intensity between stop and start. Movement maintains itself and consumes itself in time and space. Practise with an awareness of its path in time and its path in space. String your movability together with varying dynamic force and speed.

The following movements are extracted here from countless others to serve as examples.

Begin with one and add more and more physical notes until their chords swing your whole body over into space. When you feel you have arrived at the height of a crescendo diminish the movements gradually until they fade out into a standstill.

1. Stand and start slowly and gently to roll your shoulder-balls from their neutral position; in/up/neutral-out/up/neutral. In this way the movement forms a small curving swing of the horizontal figure of EIGHT.
   Enlarge the swing until the arms span the air like wings.
   Enlarge it further by swinging the upperbody forwards and backwards closing it in and opening it out.
   Allow the swing to take the weight of your body and to move it and you from the spot. Now walk forward and back.
   Strengthen the force of the impetus and let it take you further into space. Then run forward and back.
   Diminish the movements gradually until they return to their beginnings and you are quite still.

Vocalize your breathing. Think of the sounds and rhythms of the wind and the sea.

2. Walk in slow motion and gradually increase the tempo to normal speed.
   Increase the tempo more until you have to run and enlarge the run to jumping.
   Diminish the size of the movements and the speed gradually, return to slow motion and let the slowness fade into stillness.

Feel for a smooth transition from walking to running and to jumping and vice versa.

3. Run fast with small leg-movements and stop sharp.
   Run with big leg-movements and stop sharp.
   Run and jump over a high obstacle and resume the run.
   Run and jump over a wide obstacle and resume the run.
   Run and jump into a kneebend.
   Run and turn half- and full-turns when jumping into a kneebend.
Use a the rebound from the drop into the kneebend and resume the
        run and
     b stop in the kneebend, pause and speak or sing out.

4. Run for four counts, let your weight over-balance forward and
   sink to the floor.
   Move one leg forward, rise in a step-position and resume the run.
Repeat the sequence without counting and practise it as a rhythmical
phrase.

5. Walk four steps forward, lowering the knees, rounding your upperbody to your legs and tuck the neck and head well in.
   On counts of five, six, seven and eight lower the part of the spine
   between the shoulder-blades gently to the floor, roll over the
   rounded back, rise in a step-position and resume the walk.
Repeat the sequence without counting and practice it as a rhythmical
phrase.

6. Stand in a step-position, lift one leg back and roll it inwards in the
   hip-joint.
   With a quick out-rolling movement of the leg, turn half-way round
   and step, gripping the floor firmly with the foot.
   Step with the other foot forward and repeat the same turn. Start
   slowly and increase the speed. After five turns stop still and sing
   out. Then do the same with the other foot and turn into the other
   direction.

The horizontal and vertical crossbeams — downwards, upwards, sideways — forward, backwards, diagonal, and the in-turning minor and
out-turning major curves, circles and spirals form the physical range
of movement. The variations within this range are endless. Think of
movement then as a percussive action which radiates through and
from the body into space. Vibration, flow and beat extend from the
pulsation of the heart, and in- and out-going breath and the tensions
and relaxations of the body. But the actor's power may never be
found in the physical. He frees himself and his body for the communication of other matters. He works to get his body out of the way to
give way to 'the other'. Rhythm and melody are characteristics of
the personality. During physical practice rhythm and melody happen
in consequence of bodily action and temperament of your personality.
In rehearsal and performance you marry these with other actions,
rhythms and melodies. You do not free yourself for yourself. This
would be a closed circuit. Your awareness of 'otherness' opens the
possibilities for communication.

Rise from Kneeling

Walk/
Run/
Jump

Fall Backwards

Turn over and rise

7 EMPATHY

By imaginative transposition you think, feel and move from another stand-point and cast yourself into the other nature and embody it. The floor changes from wood to water or stony ground and you tread the other surface. The air changes from neutral to hot or cold, smoky or clear and you breathe the other air. By forming a mental-physical link you make 'the other' present and compel the spectator into the reality of the play. Any creatures and any motivations might come into the play and you go out to comprehend without exclusion. You venture near and far. You fall into the house next door like your drunken neighbour. You attack and kill a snake like a mongoose in the jungle. You dance as a member of the nobility of a certain society in a specific age. Ariel changes into a Harpy, Caliban is not far from the ape and Romeo dances exquisitely with Juliet. A bird-creature invites you to enlarge your arm- and neck-movements and to stalk in staccato-rhythms. A creature belonging to the cat-family asks you to make your breathing audible and to walk with big legato-strides. Some other creature informs you of actions without past or future or reasoning.
Existence is in every part belonging to the whole. Take away the nape-line of the goddess and you destroy her beauty. Change the deformed foot of the beggar and you alter his spine.
You strengthen the extensions from the centre by pruning the side-shoots and by virtue of selection and economy, concentration and attention to the smallest detail, you project and communicate meaning with the wordless power of sculpture, music and movement. Through the experience of movement you are able to contain movement and arrive at meaningful stillness. The spectator believes in your capacity to fly while you stand motionless on the ground.

The following lines from animal-poems are given here to relate poetry of words with poetry of movement. They should help to clarify by comparison but should in no way invite imitative or descriptive transposition by means of movement.

Extract from SNAKE by D. H. Lawrence

. . .

He drank enough
And lifted his head, dreamily, as one who has drunken,
And flickered his tongue like a forked night on the air,
   so black,
Seeming to lick his lips,
And looked around like a god, unseeing, into the air,
And slowly turned his head,
And slowly, very slowly, as if thrice adream,
Proceeded to draw his slow length curving round
And climb again the broken bank of my wall-face.

And as he puts his head into that dreadful hole,
And as he slowly drew up, snake-easing his shoulders,
   and entered farther,
A sort of horror, a sort of protest against his withdrawing
   into that horrid black hole,
Deliberately going into the blackness, and slowly drawing himself
   after,
Overcame me now his back was turned.

. . .

THE PANTHER by Rainer Maria Rilke translated by J. B. Leishman

His glance, so tired from traversing his cage's
repeated railings, can hold nothing more.
He feels as though there were a thousand cages,
and no more world thereafter than before.

The padding of the strong and supple paces,
within the tiniest circle circumscribed,
is like a dance of force about a basis
on which a mighty will stands stupefied.

And only now and then a noiseless lifting
of the eye's curtain, till an image dart,
go through the limbs' intensive silence drifting-
and cease for ever in the heart.

Extract from HAWK ROOSTING by Ted Hughes

I sit in the top of the wood, my eyes closed.
Inaction, no falsifying dream
Between my hooked head and hooked feet:
Or in sleep rehearse perfect kills and eat.

The convenience of the high trees!
The air's buoyancy and the sun's ray
Are of advantage to me;
And the earth's face upward for my inspection.

My feet are locked upon the rough bark.
It took the whole of Creation
To produce my foot, my each feather:
Now I hold Creation in my foot

. . .

The play informs you of the physical shape and behaviourism of certain societies in specific countries and times. The human sculpture alters in consequence of social changes and differences of belief and thought.

Professor E. H. Gombrich notes: 'When Molière's M. Jourdain wants to leave his bourgeois state behind to become a *gentilhomme*, he calls in the Masters of Music, of Dancing, of Fencing and of 'Philosophy'. We may laugh with Molière or we may feel somewhat embarrassed at his snobbery, but the fact remains that hierarchical society exacted a high entrance fee — a remodelling of the whole person to certain standards.'

Your body might need expansion when you address heaven and earth in Grecian times. When you long away from this earth into the infinity of heaven in Medieval times you might have to narrow your body and when you glorify man and this earth in the time of the Renaissance you would aim to broaden the dimensions by collecting strength to yourself. If your intention were to give the illusion of flight in the style of the Baroque, you would put the weight of your body on the point of one toe and curve outwards in a physical arabesque. From the middle of the nineteenth century into the twentieth century you might waltz and march with your body pressed into a corset and cut in half. During and after worldshaking events such as 'The Black Death' or The World Wars your dancing-movements would return to the conveniently called 'primitive' and they would move inwards, jitter, tremble, rock and roll and beat the ground.

Written and visual evidence and, above all, music, help and guide you to shape your body and to move or dance in the various styles of the times. When you collaborate with music you need to listen, find, feel and physically experience the other pulse, sound, beginnings and endings of phrases and complexities of composition in order to inspire, lead, control and transform your free movement into dancing.

Movement-practice is easily carried away by music and therefore you should work your purely physical movement without instrumental accompaniment to allow you to practise with full awareness.

Costume, make-up and mask effect yet a further transformation. The play tells you whether to reveal, by taking the mask off, or to change identity, by putting the mask on. Depth of inquiry into the play inspires, motivates and guides you.

Experiment with and explore the following lines extracted from plays which invite and allow for movement.

From PEER GYNT by Henrik Ibsen
Act V.

Scene: *Night. A moor, with pine trees. A forest fire has ravaged it.*
Charred tree-trunks can be seen for miles around. Here and
there white mist patches hug the earth. PEER GYNT *is*
running across the moor.

PEER: . . .
What is this sound of children weeping?
Weeping but halfway to song?
Threadballs are rolling at my feet —
Kicks them
Get away! You're blocking my path!

THREADBALLS (*on the ground*):
We are thoughts.
You should have thought us.
You should have given us
Little feet.

PEER (*goes round them*): I gave birth to one.
It was a monster with a twisted leg.

THREADBALLS:
We should have flown
Like children's voices.
Here we roll on the ground,
Grey balls of thread.

If you do not know the play the extract informs you that the
THREADBALLS are a reference to and accusation of PEER GYNT'S
deeds in the past.
Experiment with your body in this pre-form of being, embryo-like
rolled into a ball and find the weeping sounds. This calls for extreme
relaxation. Roll on the floor and discover the moments when your
upperbody unrolls, and speak, cry or sing the words out.

From THE WOMEN OF TROY by Euripides

HECABE: Lift your neck from the dust;   (*Strophe* 1)
Up with your head!
This is not Troy; the kings of Troy are dead:
Bear what you must.
The tide has turned at length:
Ebb with the tide, drift helpless down.
Useless to struggle on,
Breasting the storm when Fate prevails.
I mourn for my dead world, my burning town,
My sons, my husband, gone, all gone!
What pride of race, what strength
Once swelled our royal sails!
Now shrunk to nothing, sunk in mean oblivion!

How must I deal with grief?   (*Antistrophe* 1)
Hold, or give rein?
See where my outcast limbs have lain!
Stones for a bed bring sorrow small relief.
My heart would burst,
My sick head beats and burns,
Till passion pleads to ease its pain
In restless rocking, like a boat
That sways and turns,
Keeping sad time to my funereal song.
For those whom Fate has cursed
Music itself sings but one note —
Unending miseries, torment and wrong!

Troy is in ruins. Hecabe, the aged Queen of Troy, after having been dragged through the streets of the city, lies dishevelled on the ground. As she speaks she rises slowly. The speech continues for one more strophe and antistrophe at the end of which Hecabe stands with authority and says these lines:

> Come, weep with me while the smoke goes up from Troy!
> Once with cheerful Phrygian music,
> Solemn hymns and sacred dances,
> I, Queen Hecabe, Priam's sceptre in my hand,
> Led your steps and voices:
> Now the song is saddened
> To the seagull's crying round her helpless young.

Towards the end of the play Hecabe's fate is fully revealed and she tells us more about her physical state when she says:

> I call the dead, I who am near to death,
> Stretched on the soil, my hands beating the ground.
> . . .
>
> Come, trembling aged feet,
> You must not fail me now.

This needs imaginative projection into Hecabe's age and condition. It asks you to combat the fragile body and to reconcile physical weakness with inner strength and temperament.

From THE BACCHAE by Euripides

CHORUS: ...
> 'On, on! Run, dance, delirious, possessed!
> You, the beauty and grace of golden Tmolus,
> Sing to the rattle of thunderous drums,
> Sing for joy,
> Praise Dionysus, god of joy!
> Shout like Phrygians, sing out the tunes you know,
> While the sacred pure-toned flute
> Vibrates the air with holy merriment,
> In time with the pulse of the feet that flock
> To the mountains, to the mountains!'
> And, like a foal with its mother at pasture,
> Runs and leaps for joy every daughter of Bacchus.

These lines are spoken by one of the worshippers of Dionysus. They invite movements which extend from the pulsation of the heart — movements which beat and flow — burst and grow with dynamic force. In the original Greek text the rhythms change swiftly. Explore the possibilities here of syncopating movement and sound.
Professor E. R. Dodds in his introduction to the play gives these inspiring and guiding notes and quotations: 'To the Greeks of the classical age Dionysus was not solely, or even mainly, the god of wine. Plutarch tells us as much, confirming it with a quotation from Pindar, and the god's cult titles confirm it also: he is the power in the tree; he is the blossom-bringer, the fruit-bringer, the abundance of life'. Further Professor Dodds quotes Coleridge saying the creative imagination shows itself most intensely in 'the balance or reconciliation of opposite or discordant qualities', and especially in combining 'a more than usual state of emotion with more than usual order'.

From THE TEMPEST by William Shakespeare
Act II, Scene 2

CALIBAN: No more dams I'll make for fish;
            Nor fetch in firing
            At requiring;
         Nor scrape trenchering, nor wash dish:
           'Ban, 'Ban, Cacaliban
        Has a new master: — get a new man.
     Freedom, high-day! high-day, freedom! freedom,
    high-day, freedom!

This demands transformation of body and voice into this creature
which is man and not yet man. It also asks for strength and control
in losing control.
Hold or imagine you hold a heavy branch of a tree and swing it.
Turn crescendo-wise, fall and turn again and speak, sing, or 'howl'
the words.

From THE TEMPEST by William Shakespeare
Act III, Scene 3

Enter Ariel like a Harpy . . . .

ARIEL: You are three men of sin, whom Destiny, —
       That hath to instrument this lower world
       And what is in't, — the never-surfeited sea
       Hath caus'd to belch up you; and on this island,
       Where man doth not inhabit, — you 'mongst men
       Being most unfit to live. I have made you mad;
       And even with such-like valour men hang and drown
       Their proper selves.
       . . .

Agrippa describes Ariel as 'free from all gross and putrifying mass of
a body'. Here he appears in the visible shape of a birdlike creature.
His accusation of the 'three men of sin' continues for considerably
longer than the above extract. Explore the possibilities of jumping
into the attack with one leap and of holding the dramatic tension
during the whole accusation with controlled, meaningful stillness of
the bodily form.

To play is a total activity but the actor's transformation is never total. The player remains master of his playing. You command as much as you liberate. You employ your freedom of body and movement, imagination, invention and fantasy to counter-balance with control. In the sequence of the play you convince the audience that your actions and reactions happen for the first time though you are moving and speaking at a specific time and in a specific space every night of the show. A production of a play is done with and for people. There are rules of the play of giving, receiving and responding. Discipline of rehearsal and performance ask you to coordinate your movements with those of the other players and to integrate your actions with the whole. Within this order you freely give from the abundance of your existence to the vitality of the theatre.

SUMMARY FOR MOVEMENT PRACTICE

The summary can only assist your practice in general terms. Your movement practice should not exhaust you but should keep your body in the condition of equilibrium to work for you in rehearsal and performance. It is better to give thought to the need for the movement of particular parts and the whole body rather than to think in terms of the repetition of exercises. Practise the movements slowly at first with attention to detail and increase the measure when they work fluently.

The subdivisions are according to available time and space:

a daily practice for 15 minutes
b daily practice for 30 minutes
c daily practice for one hour

DAILY PRACTICE FOR 15 MINUTES

Loosening Out

Stand with your feet about 15 inches apart and breathe in. On breathing out with a sigh, let the upperbody sink forward rounding it to yourself and collapse into a kneebend. On breathing in straighten your legs and roll the vertebral column upwards.

Position yourself on hands and knees and wriggle with the spine.

Rise and stand with your feet slightly apart. Let the head sink forward, let it dangle and raise it from the back of the neck.

Pull both shoulder-balls up and let them sink slowly. Shake the shoulders, arms and hands out.

Raise the legs alternatively forward and shake them out as you let them sink.

Sit and shake your feet well out.

Sit on the floor, bend the knees and round the upperbody forward. Unroll the spine until the whole of your back touches the floor.

Lie flat and let the legs and arms slip away and outward from their joints. Spread out and rely on the support of the floor.

Rise and recall the physical condition from the horizontal when you stand upright.

Stand, breathe in and stretch yourself out from centre to finger-tips. Lower the arms, remain centrally upright, release the stretch by inwardly letting one part sink on top of the other and breathe out on 'Aaaaaaaaaaaaaaaah'. Remain still and free of all tensions and feel for the self-support of your body.

DAILY PRACTICE FOR 30 MINUTES

After Loosening Out, Practise for Elasticity

Pendulum swings

Let the head drop forward and swing it from side to side.
Raise the head and stretch it from the back.
Stand with your feet together and raise both arms. Let the spine drop forward and use the impetus of the fall of weight to swing the upperbody.
Stand with your feet apart, raise both arms and incline with the upperbody and arms to the diagonal upwards. Let the spine fall to the side and forward and use the impetus of the fall of weight to swing and carry the upperbody to the diagonal up on the other side. Do the same from and into the opposite direction.

Circular swings

Stand as before. Enlarge the impetus of the previous swing and allow the upperbody to be carried round in a full circle; left/fore/right/back/left/fore/right/up and reverse the direction.
Raise the shoulder-balls. Drop them forward and roll a full circle then drop them backward and roll a full circle: fore/up/back/down/FORE and back/up/fore/down/BACK.
Do the same circular movement with your arms.
Circle with your arms alternatively 8 times over your head and then let the arms hang loosely at your sides.

Pendulum swing

Raise one leg forward, let the weight of the thigh drop and let the impetus of the fall of weight swing the leg backwards and forwards.
Do this 8 times and change to the other leg.

Curved swing

Raise one leg turned inwards in the hip-joint, drop it and swing it inwards and outwards following the shape of the figure of EIGHT.
Do this 8 times and change to the other leg.

Circular swing

Sit and raise one foot off the floor. Let the foot drop from the ankle and roll a full circle starting inwards and a full circle starting outward; in/up/out/down and out/up/in/down/out. Do this 8 times and change to the other foot.
Stand with your feet together and raise both arms. Let the upperbody fall forward down and simultaneously drop into a kneebend.
Use the rebound of the fall to swing the upperbody up immediately and straighten the legs. Allow the spine to swing out until it is upright, lower the arms, breathe out and stand still. Feel for the elasticity of your body.

DAILY PRACTICE FOR ONE HOUR

After Loosening Out and Practising for Elasticity concentrate every day on Movability of specific parts of your body and work on Confluence of Movement and Voice

MONDAY: *Pelvis, Spine and Walking*

a Stand with your feet apart and bend the knees slightly. Drop the pelvis and move it forward and back.
b Position yourself on hands and knees and move the spine round, hollow and straight.
c Rise and stand with your feet slightly apart. Bend the knees a little, drop the pelvis and put your hands on the knees. Round the spine, hollow it and round it again and roll the upperbody upwards.
d Stand with the feet apart, drop the pelvis and lower into a deep kneebend. Round the upperbody to yourself, tuck the tail-end of the spine well in and slowly sit on the floor. Straighten the legs and unroll the spine until the whole of your back rests on the floor.
e Roll the spine up and stretch it forward.
   Stand in a step-position and start walking in slow motion. Check on the feathering movement in the centre of the spine. Increase the speed and walk, in normal tempo, forward, backward and around. Check on breathing.

TUESDAY: *Shoulders, Arms, Walking and Turning*

a Stand with your feet apart and raise the arms to the sides to shoulder-level. Turn the shoulder-balls in and out and let the arms fall.

b Raise the arms as before and turn the left shoulder-ball in and the right shoulder-ball out. Turning the right in and the left out continue to move the shoulder-balls in opposition to each other. Start slowly, then increase the tempo and let the arms fall.

c Stand in a step-position with the left foot back and the left arm raised to shoulder-level at the back. Turn the left shoulder-ball in, lower the head and breathe out. Turn the left shoulder-ball out, straighten the neck and breathe in. Make sure the upperbody remains central. Let the arm fall and change to the other arm and foot.

d Start from the same position as before with the left foot and the left arm at the back. Turn the left shoulder-ball in and on moving it out let the whole body follow its movement into half a turn and walk. Stop in a step-position with the right foot and the right arm back and do the same turning into the other direction. Make sure the neck and jaw remain free and speak as you move.

WEDNESDAY: *Hips, Legs and Turning*

Stand with the feet together. Lift and lower the legs alternatively to the front, to the sides and to the back.

Lift one leg to the side and turn it inward in the hip-joint. Turn the leg outward, stretch it and lower it into a big step to the side. Bring the leg back to the closed foot-position and do the same with the other leg.

b Lift one leg back and turn it inward in the hip-joint. Turn the leg outward in the height and let the whole body follow its movement into half a turn. Lower the leg and walk. Stop in step-position, lift the other leg back and do the same turning into the other direction.

c Lift both arms and one leg back and turn the arms and the leg inward. Turn the arms and the leg outward and let the whole body follow these opening movements into half a turn. Step out and grip the floor with the foot in front. Stand firm and sing out. Do the same with the other leg and turn into the other direction.

d Stand with your feet wide apart and raise your arms to the sides to shoulder-level. Lower the head and roll the shoulder-balls inward. Bend the knees a little and roll the legs inward. Turn arms and legs outward, straighten the legs and stretch the neck from the back. Stand and feel for the opening out of your body and lower the arms.

THURSDAY: *Knees, Kneeling, Sitting, Fall and Rise*

a Stand with your feet together and lower into a deep kneebend.
  Rise and straighten your legs well out.
  Stand with your feet apart and do the same.
  Stand with your feet in a step-position and do the same.
  Make sure the pelvis is dropped and the spine straight and relaxed
  when you practise the kneebends.

b Stand with the feet together, bend the knees and move them, the
  pelvis and the thighs forward. Lower the knees until they touch
  the floor gently and kneel. Move one leg forward, rise in a step-
  position and bring the feet together.

c Stand with the feet together and kneel as before. Lower the seat
  and the thighs to the side until they touch the floor and sit down.
  Rise to the kneeling-position, straighten to the centre and do the
  same to the other side.

d Stand with the feet together and let your weight over-balance
  forward and step out into a big stride. Lower the knee in front,
  kneel on it and sink with the upperbody forward to the floor.
  Bring the leg from the back to the front, round the upperbody,
  straighten the legs and roll the spine upward. Move the feet
  together and do the same with the other leg forward.

e Stand with the feet together and let your weight over-balance to
  the right side. Cross the left leg over the right and sink sideways to
  the floor. Round the upperbody over the left thigh, straighten the
  legs and roll the spine upward. Close the foot-position and do the
  same to the other side.

f Stand in a step-position with the left foot forward, raise the right
  arm upward and breathe in. Let the breath go with a sigh, round
  the upperbody to yourself and lower into a deep kneebend. Tuck
  the tail-end of the spine well in, lower the seat under the heel at
  the back and sit down. Roll the spine back on to the floor and
  stretch out. Roll the spine up and retrace the movements upwards
  until you stand as in the beginning of the sequence. Change to the
  other foot and arm. Do these movements fluently, slowly at first
  and increase the tempo gradually. After the last upward movement
  stretch well out in the height, lower the arm and feel for the full
  height of your body.

FRIDAY: *Feet, Hands, Walking, Running and Jumping*

a Sit and raise one foot off the floor.
   Bend the foot up.
   Bend the toes down.
   Stretch the instep.
   Bend the toes up.
   Bend the foot up.
   Shake the foot out and change to the other foot.

b Stand and raise one foot off the floor and bend it up. Touch the
   floor only with the heel, touch the floor only with the ball and
   touch the floor only with the toe. Reverse the movement by
   starting with the toe. Shake the foot out and change to the other
   foot.

c Stand with your feet together and raise the heels. Push the weight
   of your body off the floor in the order of heels, balls, toes and
   jump. Land on the floor in the order of toes, balls, heels and then
   bend the knees a little. Do the same with the feet apart.

d Sit and raise the arms to shoulder-level to the sides.
   Bend the hands downward and make fists.
   Move the hands upward, stretch the knuckles and stretch and
   spread the fingers. Loosen the hands out and drop the arms.

e Stand and breathe in. As you begin to breathe out run forward
   singing out on 'Haaaaaaaaaaaaaaaaaa' as long as your outgoing
   breath lasts.

f Walk in slow motion, and gradually increase the measure to
   normal speed. Increase the tempo further until you have to run
   and enlarge the movements to jumping. Diminish the size of
   movements and the speed gradually, return to slow motion and let
   the slowness fade into stillness. Feel for the lightness of your
   body.

THE X-RAYS

*The drawings which follow each section of the practice-
sequences give outer impressions of movements, while
the radiographs show inner actions and articulations of
movements.*

1 Spine rounding forward
2 Spine bending to the side
3 Shoulder lifted and neck-spine curved
4 Shoulder dropped and in right angle to neck-spine
5 Pelvis pushed to the side and weight transferred to
   one leg
6 Foot up, toes up – foot down, toes down
7 Fingers uncurling as hand rises

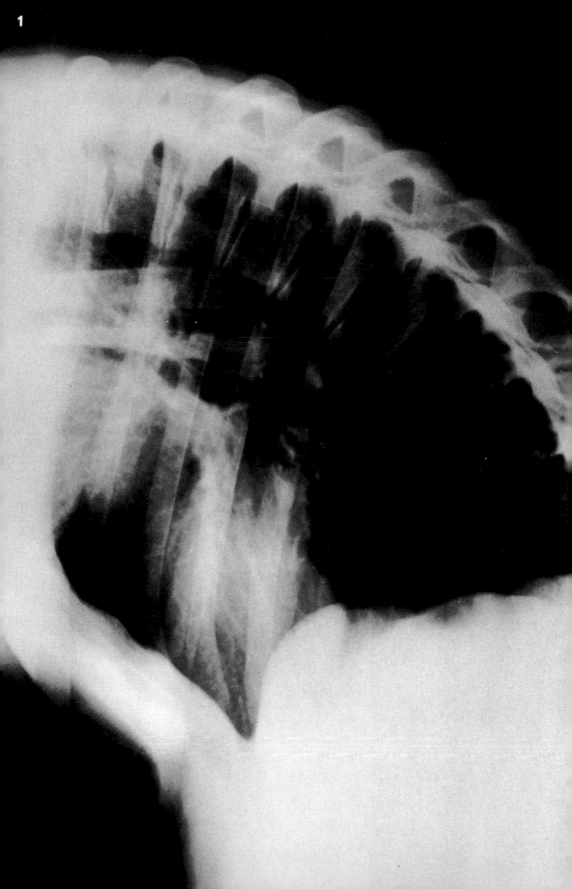

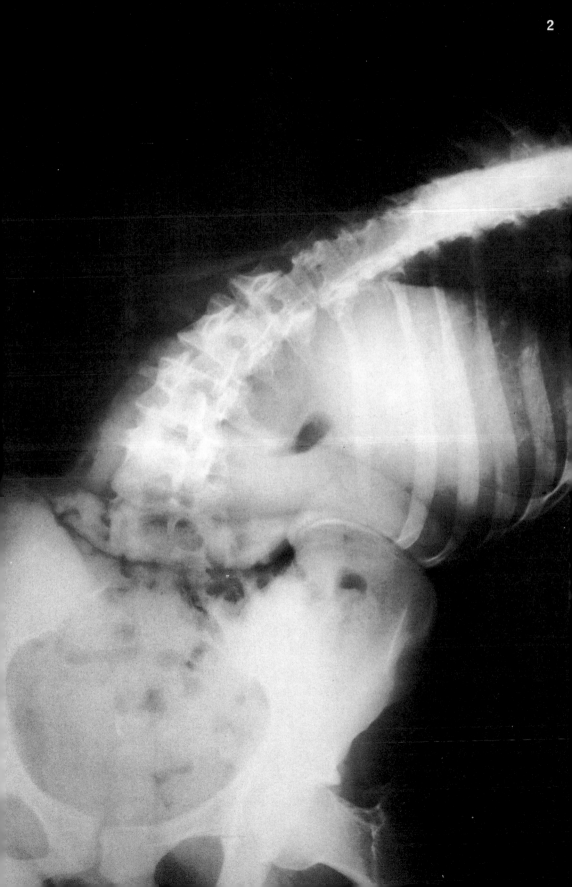

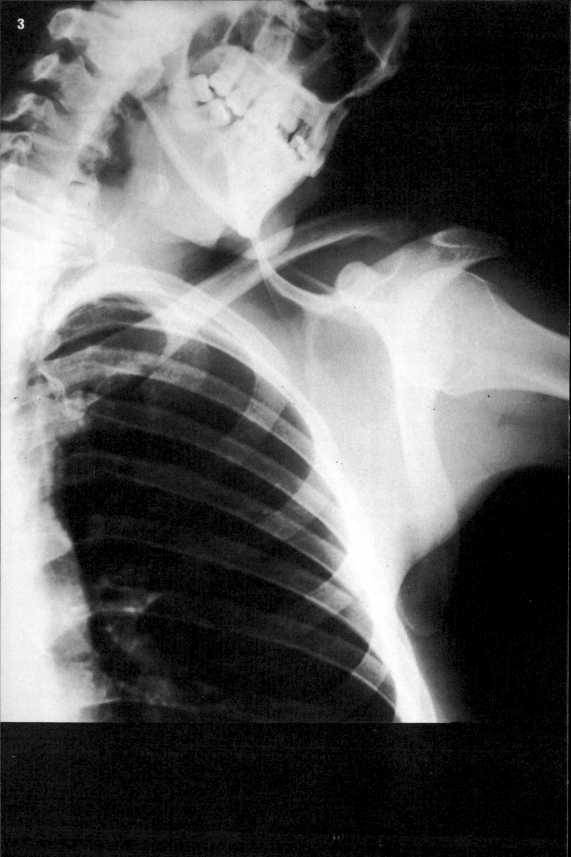

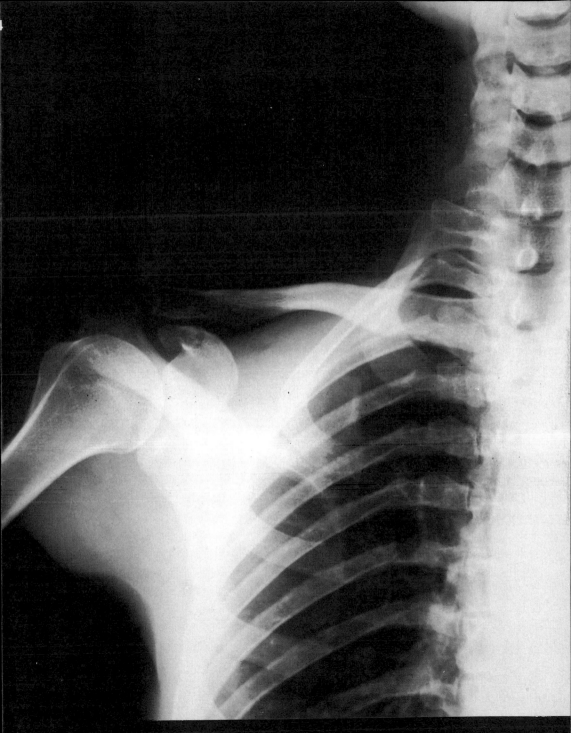

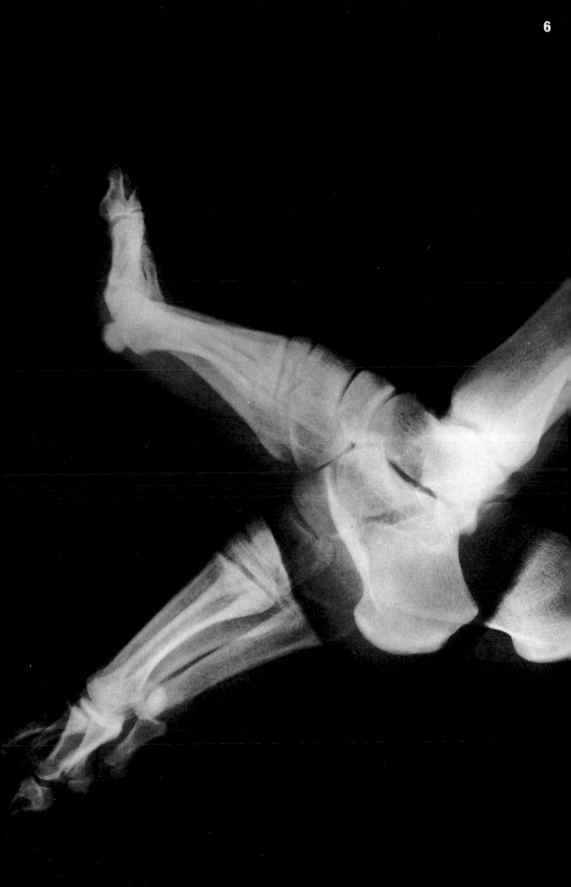

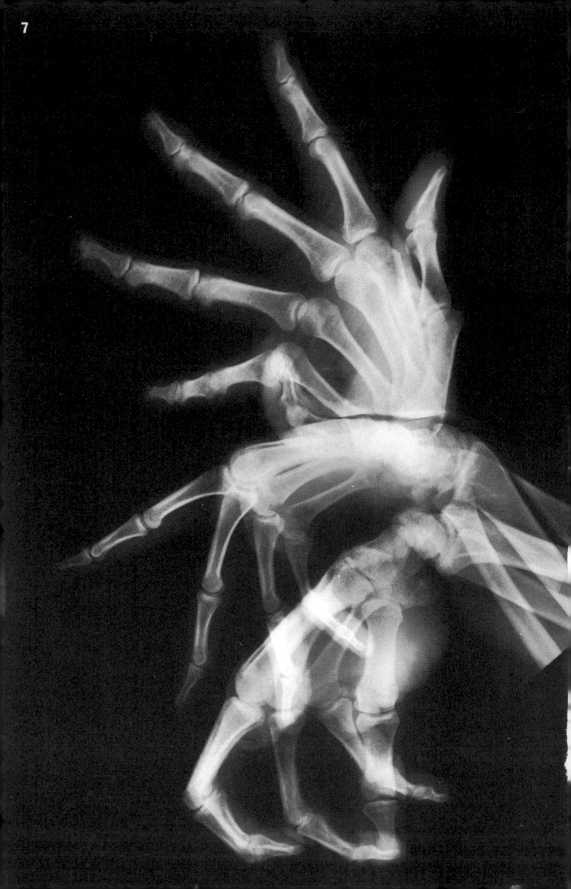